Defeating

Jezebel

**A Personal Strategy to Get Back
Under the Fountain of God's Grace**

By **Jim Banks**

Defeating Jezebel

Introduction

Over the past couple decades of ministering to broken people, my wife and I have run into more than a few people who have complained of a strained marital relationship, often augmented by prolonged financial difficulties and a general feeling of oppression. It is these few clues that hint that Jezebel may be at work. Obviously, this is not always the case, but for many, it has been the answer they have long searched for. The thing that initially threw them off track was the thought that they were doing something wrong, or their personal issues were at fault, when it really was the results of a coordinated demonic assault.

Resist the temptation to drop what you hold in your hand (or iPad/Tablet) like a hot rock because it contains the name of a spirit that's been misused and thrown around more frequently than any other. It has nothing to with your church, your opinionated mother-in-law, that pushy lady down the block, or your spouse's propensity to press you to do her bidding. I can just about guarantee that what you are about to read contains a perspective that you have not heard before, and it has been responsible for restoring hope to many because they practiced it faithfully. Not only was hope was restored in the short term, but they pressed into it they were delivered for the long term.

In many ways, what is presented here is a pattern for dealing with all manner of demonic schemes of oppression. It works for all kinds of difficulties and numerous other spiritual attacks. If you learn how it is applied in this situation, you will be able to apply it in any of the other areas in which you may need help.

It is also a portion of our own personal story, so I'm not relating something esoteric or theoretical. We lived it, and we are still applying its principles today.

I ask that if you find that what you have learned is valuable to you and your family, please pass it on to those you love, as well as those you encounter who are struggling. You will be doing them a great favor and in the process you may just save their lives and marriages.

Blessings,

Jim Banks

1

How Did We Get Here?

Several years ago, my wife went for a short visit to see a couple she dearly loved, and when she returned home, she related what she had experienced. Although these folks had been married for over fifty-five years and had lived in the same house and (I presume) slept in the same bed, they loved each other but, from my limited perspective, didn't really like each other. There just didn't seem to be any depth of relationship beyond their marital commitment to one another. As long as each fulfilled their roles, all was well.

As we discussed their situation, it became apparent that if things didn't change for us, it wouldn't take us fifty-five years to reach the same point. It wasn't that we didn't love each other, weren't committed to one another, or even argued all the time. In actual point of fact, we didn't argue at all. To the contrary, we were both active and productive in work and personal ministry, and to everyone else, we appeared to have the ideal relationship. The problem was that in many ways we were living two separate lives under the same roof.

Five years before this point, I had left a comfortable, albeit unrewarding, career as an electrical engineer to enter into the heady world of the self-employed. Three years and six months later, it proved to be the financial disaster of a lifetime, taking with it our accumulated retirement savings. The following two years were a financial roller coaster, in which we went from barely holding our heads above water to the brink of emotional and financial disaster and back again. We finally came to the realization that if we didn't get some help somewhere we were going to go down the toilet in a giant shipwreck of marriage and faith.

That's the first lesson. Before you or I can get help, we must first realize that WE need help, and want it without strings or restrictions! No matter how much my wife understands that I (we) need help, there are practically no mechanisms available to her to get me to see her viewpoint. Just because she sees we need help doesn't mean we both see it. It is imperative that we both come to the same conclusion before help can be sought. The same is true for those who you know who have problems. They cannot be helped until they are ready for it.

One cannot determine for the other that he or she needs help and set about to arrange it. It's rather like taking a stubborn dog to obedience training. You can drag it there, but there is absolutely no guarantee that anything positive is going to happen.

For those of you who know that your marriage needs help because you are having relational issues, do not wait until both of you come to the conclusion that something needs to be done. By then it may be too late. Go now for yourself. The reality is that we bring us and our baggage from our family or origin into the marriage and often that baggage is really toxic. This is especially

true if you left home or got married because you could
no longer stand it at home. Go get help now! Because I
can guarantee you that half of your spouse's issues are
yours. If you can get your issues resolved, then more
than half of your spouse's issues will evaporate. He or
she will then come to appreciate the benefit of what
you've done and may decide to go for help of their own
accord.

You know, it's a funny thing about finances . . . the lack
thereof has the ability to pressurize every other aspect
of our lives. Unfortunately, it is often only the lack of
financial flexibility that motivates us to do something
about it. This was one of the greatest motivating factors
in us deciding to look for help.

2

The Common Issues

Like so many others before us, the combination of relational isolation, continuing monetary problems, and the inability to find a way out of it, a clear pattern began to emerge that led us to the conclusion that Jezebel and its minions were at work ... but only after we were taught to see the signs.

For others, additional clues might include: separation between spouses, which can include sexual difficulties; communication issues, prolonged financial difficulties, which I describe as a hole in the bucket where income is never enough to make it and just when it looks like you are about to get ahead an unexpected expense jumps up and consumes it; oppressive debt; control issues; relational isolation, loss of communication; lack of clarity (or confusion) on many issues; seemingly locked in a spiritual wilderness; prolonged health problems; depression, including altered or disturbed sleep patterns; isolation; issues of pride and selfishness surfacing between spouses; self-pity and an abiding sense of hopelessness; a series of poor decisions; an apparently out-of-control or uncharacteristic dedication to a hobby or the television; and a decided passivity in both praying and fighting the enemy.

The bottom line is that in all of these situations, believe it or not, the result is a form of idolatry that has silently crept in without your knowledge. What has occurred over time is a slow transference of trust from God to self. And if someone has been in this situation for some time, they will have stopped off along the way and trusted in credit cards or finance companies or a property's equity. They have lost the hope that God would come through. Because this is idolatry, Deuteronomy 28 defines the curse associated with it as *poverty*. Consequently, they are out of the "place of grace," and that means that nothing they try will work.

In a nutshell, that's what had happened to us.

3

So Who's Responsible?

To learn about how Jezebel works, let's start in 1st Kings 18. Jezebel had installed the worship of two foreign Gods in Israel and in order to make way for them she had killed a bunch of the Lord's priests. In a half-hearted attempt at retaliation, her husband Ahab, the erstwhile King of Israel, had unsuccessfully chased Elijah all over the countryside trying to add him to the list. Due to the Lord's protection he was never able to catch up with him. The Lord had prophetically revealed all of Ahab's plans to capture him to Elijah, and Ahab and Jezebel were quite frustrated as a result. Tired of the whole game himself, (1Kings 18:10-13) Elijah confronted Ahab face-to-face, but once face-to-face Ahab could only muster a pathetic insult: *"there you are . . . you troubler of Israel!"* (1 Kings 18:17) (KJV). What a weenie!

Assuredly, the nation of Israel wasn't troubled about where Elijah was—Ahab was because of his frustration (and his wife's insistence.) It had gotten so bad that if someone thought they had seen him somewhere and Ahab couldn't find him, Ahab killed the messenger who made the report. Consequently, and understandably, absolutely no one was the least bit interested in reporting anything about Elijah's whereabouts.

When Elijah confronted Ahab face-to-face, the natural assumption would be that because he was so mad Ahab would try to kill Elijah. But oddly enough there is no record that Ahab even waved so much as a toothpick at Elijah during their encounter. He stood there dumbfounded as Elijah turned the tables, stating that Ahab and his forefathers have been the real troublers of Israel because they had totally forsaken the commandments of the Lord, which was indeed true. A major reason behind this shift in affections of the nation was the Sidonian princess Ahab had married, who came to town with all her strange gods in tow.

Elijah then commanded Ahab to gather all of Israel for a big face off, including the priests of the foreign gods that Jezebel had set up, which was preceded by Elijah challenging the people:

> *"How long will you limp between two opinions? Either God is God, or Baal is god. Which is it?"* (1 Kings 18:21) (KJV)

This is actually the root issue that God wants to deal with in all of us. We're not so dumb as to go to a store and a select an idol off the shelf to worship, but we do it nonetheless in many other more subtle ways. We whip out a credit card. We're in charge. Because we worship independence and self-determination, we choose to make all the decisions. We determine where all our time is spent and what it is spent on—even if it's just reading e-mail, looking at Facebook, Twitter, Instagram, watching Youtube videos or just mindlessly Googling interesting stuff on the net. If we get busy enough, we might not even have time to think about God at all, much less any of our own personal issues.

Elijah entered the contest on Mount Carmel with the prophets of Baal and Asherah to determine who was Lord over the nation. The people were double-minded. Through Elijah, God brought them to a clear place of choice in each of their lives.

God defied all human reasoning at this point. It was Elijah against 850—impossible odds in the natural. However, the people needed to get "un-halted"! (Halt means to walk with a limp or become lame; to stand in doubt between two courses or paths; to display weakness or imperfection; to put things on hold; to cease marching or journeying; or to discontinue or terminate a project for lack of funds.)

We have made much of the power of unity—and there is power in it - but we have thought that that power was derived from a decision to unite with others, when in actuality the power of unity comes when we are unified in what God told us to do. That same power exists for you when the only two who are in agreement are you and the Lord. God doesn't care that the odds against you are 850:1. When you're on His side, the odds could be "a bazillion to one"—you will still win!

In 1 Kings 18:40, Elijah dispatched the 450 priests of Baal and the 400 priests of Asherah. God even showed off a bit before them all by answering Elijah's prayer and appearing with a pillar of fire and consuming a huge sacrifice—the wood and the water, the rocks and all. At the end of the big show, Elijah rounded up all the priests and beheaded them all with a sword. Then he made it rain. This was the same guy who three years before had prophesied that it would not rain for three years and the heavens had shut up completely. God showed off again!

If that were not enough, Elijah outran the King's chariot, obviously outfitted with the fastest horses in the land, on foot, back to the city of Jezreel a distance of about 18 miles. Because Ahab was a tad on the prideful side I'm sure he didn't take the loss in stride. When he got home he was a little on the huffy side.

We are about to witness a transition of a power struggle. To this point Elijah has only been a thorn in the side of the king and queen, but this went from being a confrontation to a major retaliation on the part of a higher order demonic entity in an attempt to punctuate the loss with a victory, one which hopefully would dissuade the people from overturning all the progress Jezebel had previously made. In many cases this is the sort of counter-attack that you and I can experience following a major victory of our own. So pay attention to what comes next.

The story of the counter-attack unfolds for us in the first four verses of 1 Kings 19. Scripture tells that Ahab told his wife Jezebel about all the things that Elijah had done. Notice that he mentioned absolutely nothing about what God had done, but only what Elijah had done to her personally appointed priests. He didn't mention anything about the confrontation over the wet sacrifice, nothing about the futility of the priests she had caused to be set in place, nothing about the humiliation heaped upon the gods she served and had caused Israel to serve, and nothing about the fact that Elijah had made it rain again. Nor did he mention the fact that Elijah had given him and his chariot a head start but had still beaten him back to the city on foot.

What he did relate to her probably went something like this:

"Hon, I've got good news, and bad news! The good new is we're going to have a lot more time with just each other around dinner time! And some wonderful budget relief from those normal Wednesday night dinners. The bad news is that you have a lot fewer friends now . . . in fact there will be 850 fewer of them. They are all dead. Not sure who's gonna bury them all. Guess I'll have to take care of that in a day or two. It's gonna be hard figuring out which head goes with which body.

Do you remember Bobby, that cute, baby-faced little priest you liked so much? You know, the one who used to sit three seats to the left of you at dinner every Wednesday night? Come to think of it, he was the one who gave you that cute little black kitten for your birthday last year. Well, you just won't believe what happened to that poor thing. Elijah was getting so tired swinging that big heavy sword that he just couldn't get the job done on Bobby quickly. He had to hack on him three or four times. Even stopped once to catch his breath before he finished him off . . . What agony he must have been in . . . poor fellah!"

What was at work here was a serious case of pride. Things were certainly going badly for the home team, but there was no mention of what God had done nor any mention of what He might do. There was only talk *of the results* of the day's events. There was no question on

Ahab's lips about what this might mean to them or how their behavior might have to change to accommodate these events—nor one thought given to what God might be saying through this event to the nation's leaders.

Now, as we are going through the balance of this account I want you to put yourself in this man's (Elijah's) shoes because what I'm going to teach you is one of the major keys about dealing with the issues that confront you and your family personally. It's also a significant key that is useful in fighting any kind of a spiritual attack that comes against you. It has become one of the most important tools that my wife and I have learned in all our days of following Christ in that it reminds us where He is supposed to be in our lives and gives us a very practical means of measuring the effects when we have allowed other influences to usurp that place.

4

A Little Background

The reality is that you and I have an enemy in this world. I invite you to go to our ministry website www.houseofhealingministries.org and on the "Home" page there's a video that gives a lot of background about who your enemy really is and how it came to be. But to give you the 25 cent version, there was a war in heaven. Lucifer got booted out and had to do a serious face-plant on Earth. When he dusted himself off he was most than a little offended, he was seriously ticked off. He was ticked off at God. He was also irritated at you because he knew you were coming, and why you were coming.

In Genesis Chapter one, we read that God created us in His image. In John Chapter four we read that God is a spirit and those who would worship Him must worship Him in spirit and in truth. In Jeremiah Chapter one, we get a little bit more insight, not only about Jeremiah himself but also about you and I individually. In Jeremiah, 1:5, we read that Jeremiah said,

> *"the Lord told me that before He formed me in my mother's womb that He knew me and He set me apart to be a prophet to the nations and established me for that very thing."* (my paraphrase)

This verse is important for several reasons, but the first is the implication that before recorded history, you and I, as spirits beings, had some kind of undefined relationship with God. The King James Version the wording is very interesting when it says, *"The Lord said that before He formed me in my mother's womb, he knew me."* That word Hebrew translated as "knew" is the same word that is used when Adam *"knew"* Eve and she conceived a son. The implication is clear.

The cool thing about this passage, although it accurately describes Jeremiah, it also it is applicable to each one of us. It declares that Jeremiah, and I believe each one of us, was created with a specific purpose in God's eternal scheme, a specific time and place, and a specific thing to do. Ephesians 2:10 also declares that there are good works established for you to perform before the foundation of the world. There are things that have been established for you to accomplish.

Do you remember the verse that says, *"Delight yourself in the Lord and He will give you the desires of your heart."* I believe that all of the desires that were placed in your heart are consistent with the purpose for which you were created. I repeat … you and I had specific things poured into us as spirits when we were created by God; everything we needed that was coincident and consistent with our purpose. And this includes our intellect, talents, skills, abilities, our temperament, our curiosity, gifts (natural and spiritual), whatever.

I believe that it was on the occasion of our creation as individuals that there was a witness to each one. At the time that witness was probably marveling at the diversity, the uniqueness and the range of creativity being displayed. That witness was Lucifer and he remembers why you and were made. It was awesome to watch back then but it's not good news to him now, the shoe is on the other foot.

When Lucifer got major demotion he also got a name change; it is now satan (or the devil.) He took up his position here on Earth, and he is called, the prince of the power of the air. He is the guy who's in charge of the atmosphere of the Earth.

You and I, once upon a time, apparently had some kind of significant relationship with the Lord, but when began our tour of duty on Earth, we started off in the womb of a woman, but the thing that was missing was this ability to connect with the Lord on the same level as before. Why was that? Because satan knew what God had in mind for you and I, and in order to try to interrupt or cancel that plan satan had to mess with our personal identity. He had to wound us. He had to bring trauma into our lives, along with affliction, torment, and terror so that we would do something that Elijah did to himself, noted in 1 Kings Chapter 19.

You and I respond to negative situations in a manner that are very common to man. When stuff comes at us, the first thing we do is try to defend ourselves – self protection or preservation. One of the primary schemes of the enemy is to get you to stop living out of your heart; to not live through who you were created to be but to live life out of your head where the natural instinct of self-preservation are located. There, you have to assess everything for its ability to harm you, for its ability to shortcut something of your own plans. We become defensive. As a result you have to assess everything for its ability to harm you or cause you loss and create a scheme to deal with it, including a backup plan in-case that one doesn't work.

What we are doing, then, is choosing to defending ourselves. In effect, I am choosing to become my own god. Since I am normally given to presume that I am the only resource at my disposal, I'm in charge of everything. Sly program, isn't it? And it works for almost every one of us.

One of the other things about the enemy is that he is extraordinarily sly. Very seldom does the enemy come to you face to face in a confrontation as he did with Elijah, but wants to sneak up on you, surreptitiously, secretly, silently. After a period of time, you find yourself up to your hips in alligators and you cannot figure out what the heck happened so you will respond just as Elijah did.

5

Back to Our Story

In 1 Kings 19:1 we read,

And Ahab told Jezebel all that Elijah had done.

He was speaking strictly from the flesh; a man who has no spiritual discernment or comprehension whatsoever. What he had done is bought into the system of the world itself which says, "My personal interests are the only thing that matters. What I feel or sense, if anything, really doesn't count. All that spiritual stuff is for the priests. I will do as I please."

Being a non-spiritual man I don't believe that Ahab felt he had a stake in this battle at all, in spite of the fact that he was the King and the ultimate responsibility for the direction of the nation fell at his feet. Since he didn't set up this new religious order he had no skin in the game – nothing to lose. **Selective responsibility** is a self-inflicted curse. It's not a mystery that we can't see what's going on when we refuse to see.

And also how he had executed all of the prophets by the sword.

Obviously, his passive-aggressive nature paid off in his

eyes. Certainly, this was big deal that somebody needed to respond to, after all there were now 850 dead people somebody had to deal with. He could see that this was a big deal in the local "spiritual realm" but since it didn't bother him he had to make sure that those who cared were caught up on current events. We see the results of his ploy unfolding in verse 2.

> *"Then Jezebel sent a messenger to Elijah saying, "So let the gods do to me and more also if I do not make your life as one of them by this time tomorrow."*

Now the interesting thing about this in my view, is Jezebel is probably a principality. If not a principality, then certainly a higher ordered demonic entity for you will notice that it wasn't she who delivered the message of a declaration of war, but one of her underlings.

It is not first the spiritual then the natural, it is the natural then the spiritual. (1 Corinthians 15:46) I think that part of the understanding of that is this: if you want to see how things operate and are structured in the demonic arena, you have to look in the natural arena. Look at how is an army structurally created. It's a pyramidal thing; one big guy at the top and a bunch of little guys at the bottom and a few slightly higher ranked guys in between.

If, for whatever reason, the president of Venezuela decided to attack you personally, what would he do? I can tell you what he wouldn't do. He wouldn't get a flight to Miami, catch a connecting flight to the city nearest you, call a cab and drive up in the middle of the night, pull his sword out, beat on your door and call you out into the street to fight him. Not even a remote possibility!

He would stand on the capitol steps of Caracas in all the finery he could muster and declare to the whole world how things would be much better off if you were deceased, a blight removed from the face of the earth. In so doing, he would declare war against you and he would send some privates, a few sergeants, maybe even some officers to dispatch you.

Now we know a couple of things. In Psalms 115:16 the word says this:

> The Heavens are the Lord's Heavens and the Earth He has given into the hands of men. (Psalms 115"16)

From that, we deduce that through the name of our Lord Jesus Christ, we have authority over demonic entities that impact the earth, but there is some realm in this pyramidal scheme above which we can't deal with them. That's above our pay grade, above our authority. We have to ask the Lord to deal with them.

In this particular case, Jesus hadn't shown up yet, so that wasn't an option, however, it seems that Elijah didn't choose to call on God at all. What we see here is an official spiritual war that was declared and initiated by Jezebel.

What I want you to do for the next few minutes is put yourself in Elijah's place. What would you be thinking? What would you be feeling? What would you be experiencing? I'm going to tell you, this is exactly what you and I have to deal with.

One of the interesting things about this encounter is that in spite of the fact that Jezebel declared war against Elijah, there is nothing anywhere in scripture that says Jezebel did anything about it. In other words, she didn't raise a rabble from the streets to do her dirty work, she didn't call for some palace guards, she didn't even ask her hubby for a cadre of secret assassins. She didn't do anything about her threat. Yet, all hell broke loose against him.

We read in verse three:

> And when he <u>saw that</u>, he arose and ran for his life. (KJV)

This is some very interesting phraseology. When someone yells at you it isn't normally accompanied by a visual of each word being launched at you. However, Jezebel painted the picture of what she wanted to happen quite vividly in Elijah's mind and it's quite obvious that Elijah got the message in living color because the images of what had occurred to the slain priests of her false gods were still fresh in his mind since they were still less than 24 hours old.

Now the first thing that gets launched against you following a declaration of spiritual war, as it did against Elijah, is **intimidation**. When we are faced with a problem of any magnitude, the enemy immediately comes to try to make that problem look much bigger than it actually is. For most of us, our minds can quickly go to extremes because we're trained by the world to do that. Any little bitty thing can be stretched into losing your job, your life savings, your house, the car, a good credit rating, etc. That's the attack of the enemy against each and every one of us, blow it up so that it looks overwhelming, minimizing our ability and our resources.

Its goal is to **touch any personal insecurities** you may have and turn them into a potential for complete disaster.

Our natural response to traumatizing situations that threaten our lives is to trigger our most primitive responses to imminent danger; freeze, fight or flee. What it did to Elijah was to effectively freeze him from engaging in what should have been a natural thought for a spiritual man, instead there was apparently no thought to stop for a moment and ask the Lord to intervene. He was in full-on panic mode which compelled him to flee the peril.

So it could easily be said that intimidation's strategy is to get you to quickly respond in the flesh without thinking, for if you take a minute and respond in the spirit, its game-over.

That first ploy is invariably followed by the attack of another lower order demonic entity called **confusion**. Its job is the same as its name, create confusion while you are still being ministered to by intimidation. Its purpose is to effectively cloak from your view any potential a way to solve this problem. The handle to grab hold of this thing is obscured for you. There doesn't seem to be a way to escape it, or get around it. Somehow or another we are going to have to deal with it but seemingly all potential solutions are masked so that there is no clarity of action to be seen.

What that typically does is mess with our sense of personal security and safety. We can confidently handle just about anything when we have plan firmly in place. Not so when the solution is just out of our grasp.

That's what happened to Pat and I when we were attacked by this thing. We thought we had considered everything to get out of our dilemmas and yet in every one of them there seemed to be some reason we couldn't engage it. Even when we tried something else to make additional money it would never produce it fast enough to make the effort pay off, all the while growing and accelerating our anxiety because there was no answer.

When intimidation and confusion get us off balance our natural reaction is **fear**. Fear is one of the most interesting things about the enemy's strategy and it is generally the most effective of all his weapons for it is his principle and he never uses it sparingly.

When Jesus Christ died, buried, was resurrected, and sat down at the right hand of the Father, that process did one thing. Satan himself was judged. In John 12:31 Jesus says,

> *"Now is the judgment of this world: now shall the prince of this world be cast out.*

Meaning that satan himself was booted out of the world, where he was originally sent when he was thrown out of heaven following his rebellion against God. He's been removed – prevented from attacking you in person. To make a point of it all, in that process another very important thing happened,

> *"He (Jesus) paraded his victory, taking captivity captive."* Ephesians 4:8

Essentially what he (Jesus) did was to strip away from every power, every ruler, and every principality, all weapons of its warfare. The only thing that the enemy has left to use against us is fear and deception and he's really good at using both against us.

It is easy for us to get into fear because for most of us we've seen trouble before and we know what it is and we can smell it a mile away. But when it is preceded by intimidation and the spirit of confusion, it looks like we don't have a way out of this thing, we begin to fear. And since we always go to extremes when fear arrives, we fear for our lives.

Jesus even foretold it when he said,

> *"In the world ye have tribulation; but be of good courage (fear not): I have overcome the world.* (John 16:33 Darby)

Although we have no promise of tomorrow, in this day and age, you and I don't have to deal everyday with the fear that we will lose our lives, as those before us who had to deal with wars, invasions, famines and plagues. But we have no end of stimulus to fear a lot of other thing; Cancer, Fear of losing relationships. Fear losing our jobs or livelihood, our positions, the loss of our lifestyle, our homes, our health, etc. Fear is a very common thing for us and it's one of the easiest things for the enemy to push the button. I don't know about you, but when tribulation came knocking on my door, I used to always go to fear ... and in doing so I never got to the One who overcame it all and could help me do the same.

Consequently, for those of us who have been trained by the world to choose fear first what we do next is just what Elijah did? It says:

v.3, He arose and ran for his life and went to Beersheba.

Beersheba is about forty miles south of Jerusalem and if you've ever been in that country it's pretty rugged. Fear causes us to do the very same thing that he did. Since our natural God-given survival instincts are either fight, flight or freeze, we often choose to run away from our problems. We stuff the fear. We stuff the pain. We stuff our fear of the consequences. We don't really want to deal with them. That is the very thing that the enemy wants to have happen to us, because if I choose to live life out of my head and shut my heart down to isolate myself from feeling pain, then I have a really difficult time connecting with the Lord, who said, *"Cast all your cares on me because I care for you."* (1Peter 5:7)

Note in verse 3 above it says that he ran for his life. When fear hits us that strongly we make some very **poor decisions,** and I will touch on this later.

We have read recently of those who had to rapidly evacuate because the roaring flames of the out-of-control Carr fire near Redding, CA (August 2018) were quickly advancing upon their homes licking up everything in its path. In their haste they left behind some very valuable things they wish they hadn't; phones, medications, laptops, even wallets and second vehicles. They had no time to think about what they might need over the next couple of weeks, and it was plenty for many because the fire took 1,077 homes. When your life is in immediate peril and death is advancing quickly it's too late to plan. You grab what's right in front of you at the time and run – another ministry of confusion driven by fear.

To insure the enemy gets the response he's after the next little bugger he sends out against us is **Isolation**. What we typically do is run from the Lord instead of to Him. When we run, it's just not into the next room, it's to the next town, next county.

When we face significant problems in life, and particularly if they persist for a while, we begin to isolate for a multitude of reasons. We don't want to have to explain our selves again, tell the story once again of our failure to get a grip on things.

We don't want to be reminded of our **powerlessness** in the situation because it touches something we all hate. The world has taught us that, *"If I do right, everything will be right."* And when things are wrong, then either I've done something wrong ... or God forbid, I am wrong. (That is to say, something's wrong with me.) So we will keep our distance from people who might accidentally remind us of the possibility.

Another reason is that our society values independence and self reliance. So when there's nothing you can do about your marginalizing circumstance we think that asking for help is admitting defeat, so it's somehow more noble to suffer than to admit we need help.

Another contributing factor to a decision to isolate is because of our performance orientation we think that somehow ee could have prepared for this; we should have seen it coming and at least been able to mitigate the losses were are faced with. It plays on our pride.

Now there's another strategy behind the specific attack of isolation. We were created for relationship. It is a foundational driving force in every human being. We crave the company of other people for their touch (physical and emotional support). Human touch is the universal language of acceptance. Isolation robs us of it, especially when it is of our own volition.

You see, each one of us needs people in our lives. Especially one or two of them who are close enough to walk up to us and kick us in the shins (even in the midst of our grief) and say, "Hey, that's the dumbest thing I've heard you say in a long time. You may need to rethink that." That may be the last thing we want to hear, but that is precisely what we need to hear when we need it. Isolation prevents natural correction offered by those who care about us.

What does Elijah do here? He's not only running for fear of his life, but he's **abandoning his place**. Elijah was an interesting character. Elijah was a Levite, so he had a piece of property and a dwelling, probably even a garden, but he was also the head of the School of The Prophets, so he had access to about 400 young men who would have laid down their lives for him. He had resources that he never used. He was a well known, understood to be the prophet to the nation of Israel. In fact, even other nations knew of this man. At a minimum, he could have run to the local synagogue and clung to the altar, which is understood in almost any culture to be a place of sanctuary, even for murderers. And yet he did none of the above.

What happens to us when we decide to retreat from difficult situations? When we step out of our defined place – the place of God-ordained authority that He gave us, we **surrender our authority** to the enemy. That, in and of itself, is one of the greatest travesties of our lives. Essentially what we're doing is willfully bowing to defeat. Something none of us ever wants to do, but this is something that we normally do, even as he did, because after all, Elijah was a normal guy. Yes, he had special gifting and a special place in the nation of Israel, but we have them too. Yet, he gave up the very place that he was supposed to be operating in even in the face of direct opposition by a secular authority.

When you give up your spiritual authority in response to a secular attack, the only remaining weapons you have are secular as well.

Now let's take this a step further. Interestingly enough, Elijah had plenty of provision; the 400 young men from the School of the Prophets for support, the Show Bread upon the temple Altar, his own garden, etc. So what did he do? He willingly walked out of his place of provision into a place of **poverty and lack** – another ministry of Jezebel. If you agree with it, what does it do? It ministers evil to you.

If I were to walk up to you, smile sweetly, then reach around and pull your wallet out of your pocket, and you didn't stop me, what you would be doing is to give me tacit approval to minister evil to you.

This is essentially what happened here. Elijah never fought, never said no, never disagreed, never put up so much as an objection about anything. He fell to the ministry of every demonic entity that's been unleashed by the authority, Jezebel that was arrayed against him.

And then scripture tells us Elijah decided to leave his servant there. This was a bondservant. One of the things that follows when we begin isolating or separating from people, is we always comes to that place of **separating from covenant relationships**.

These relationships may be covenant relationships with your spouse or family members. These are the people that typically love us and care about us the most. And yet, because we're embarrassed about the situation and we don't have an answer for it, this is what we do. And these things hurt us – and them.

This was part of the struggle my wife and I encountered. About a year before we got to this point in our lives we had finally folded an unsuccessful a business we were in. The following year was a real struggle, and although the basic bills were being paid there was never any surplus. Our bucket had a hole in it. When it appeared that there might be a surplus, something would break; the washing machine, a car repair, something, would eat it up. This kind of **stress** over an extended period of time wears on a marital relationship and isolation begins to creep in. It certainly did with us.

Even though we were still sexually active, the level of our communication (and consequently, the intensity of our relationship) had slowly devolved to answering the question, "What do we need to do to get through this day or this week?" Simply the minimum. When financial stress lingers for more than a few months things get tough because the two of you have already searched for every solution; you have discussed part time jobs, talked about starting a new company, investigated the availability of a new job, heck, even applied for a few and you have thoroughly discussed what everyone else is doing. We had even considered selling stuff to generate some extra cash, but we were always stymied by the fact that we didn't have that much to sell and what we did have to sell wasn't worth much. So the feelings (dare I say, demons) of **helplessness** and **hopelessness** begin to pile on as well.

In the beginning of verse four we find;

He, himself, went a day's journey into the wilderness.

Before we get to the point about wilderness all by itself, I think we have to look at the tail end of the previous sentence and the first five words of this sentence. The pressure that a significant spiritual attack creates causes us to make some pretty bone-headed decisions and if you look at what Elijah did here he's made a number of them in a row. We could ascribe his reactions to fear alone, as well as to the cumulative impact of all these lower order demonic spirits that were unleashed in a coordinated attack against him. Each of us might respond differently to this sort of challenge if we were to be put in his shoes, some even worse, so my guess is that Elijah had perhaps crossed swords with Jezebel before and was well aware of her tendency to extremism, which was certainly something to be concerned about.

In his haste to hi-tail it out of town, he took no provision; food, water, clothing.) He probably even considered perhaps for a moment that he may never be able to come back here again. He's knows that he's headed for the wilderness where it will be really hard for anyone to find him and they'll be no random witnesses to rat him out. But the wilderness is hot as the hinges of hell in the daytime and as cold as a refrigerator at night and still he doesn't stop to pick up an extra cloak to shield him from the heat of the sun, nor fend off the cold at night.

The thing that caught my attention is the tendency we have when faced with what is deemed to be an overwhelming challenge is our bent motivation to go-it-alone. It seems that when we respond to isolation with any level of agreement it always pushes us to the extreme end of that agreement as it meets with some desire for **martyrdom**, which is born of feeling sorry for ourselves. We certainly don't want our personal challenges to be the source of collateral damage in the lives of the innocent bystanders we care about, but that's what friends are for. Scripture even tells us that "*a brother is born for adversity.*" (Psalms 17:17) ... and "*there is a friend that sticks closer than a* *brother.*" (Proverbs 19:24) The source is our own **independent spirit** that we have partnered with since we were children.

What we have to understand is that there is a major ulterior motive behind all this. The name Jezebel means "non-cohabitant or un-married." The sole goal of this higher order demonic spirit is to get you to sever every life giving relationship you have, and isolation and severing covenant relationships are only steps toward the real goal, getting you to separate even from God.

One of the favorite schemes of the enemy is to *"wear out the saints."* (Daniel 7:25) and it uses our own pathetic reasoning to do it. When a major financial tribulation visits us we respond by fighting the enemy as we should, then we turn to God and ask for some help in the battle. If nothing changes we go back and fight the enemy some more, then turn a beg God to engage in the fight. When nothing positive happens we wave our sword at the enemy some more, then make demands of God out of our frustration. Finally, we give up both activities because we don't want to be disappointed anymore that both our warfare and our prayers are to no avail. (Probably more of the lies of "If I do right, everything will be right" mindset.) The point being that we **voluntarily lay down our weapons**.

I had a happily married friend once who was going through long season of financial hell at one point in his life and he said, "I'd even repent of homosexuality if I thought it would change the situation." Once again the result of the viewpoint of "If I do right, everything will be right" so if God isn't fixing the problem I need figure out what I did wrong, then I can fix it and everything will be well again.

Back to verse four;

He, himself, went a day's journey into the wilderness.

The word 'wilderness' is code for separation from God. It's an isolation that has come physically and emotionally, but it becomes an isolation of the heart as well. This is one of the most devastating things that we can do. What we do is willfully shut down the place where the Lord can speak to us, even in the midst of the trouble where I need Him to speak to me. By making this choice we have effectively closed our ears and closed our heart to the greatest resource in the universe, but we don't really know that we are doing it. This is just a natural progression of what we typically do because in my heart-of-hearts I am afraid that what I'll hear God say is, 'This is all your fault, you dummy." Which another ramification of our performance orientation that we learned from the world.

   "Wilderness" is a great Biblical code word. It is a place where the noise of our own defeat tends to drown out the *"still small voice of God."* It is where we become so absorbed by our circumstances that, like Gahazai, we can't see that *"more are they that are with us than they that are against us."* (2 kings 6:16) And the promises of Hosea 2:4 and Job 35:15 cannot be seen because "there is none so blind as he who will not see."

Back to our story; You have to remember that the stress he's under wears quickly on his energy levels. (You and I are no different, although he's probably in better physical condition than most 21st Century couch potatoes due to having to walk everywhere.) The adrenaline surge he experienced when the bad news came took a bunch of it too. Then on the heels of that he troops about 40 miles the first day, which at a pace of five miles per hour makes that a solid eight hours of hoofin it on a smooth road with no stops. And soon we'll see that he does it again for a second straight day, this time through a landscape that looks more like the jagged rock covered surface of Mars than a sand-strewn desert. At some point exhaustion begins to set in, which doesn't bode well for making good decisions either, which have been in short supply during the last 48 or so.

Scripture in verse 4 then informs us that:

He came and sat down under a broom tree.

I don't know if you've ever seen a broom tree, it's not really a tree, it's more like an overgrown bush or shrub. It is also known as a juniper. It is a member of the cypress family and initially has needles for leaves, which become scales as they mature. If you have seen cedars along US highways you can picture what a juniper looks like. We also find them employed as a privacy fence when planted relatively close together.

It is not really meant for shade, but you can use it for whatever shade it produces if you have nothing else to look to. Because of its needles it's not very cuddly so leaning up against it to take full advantage of whatever level of shade it provided would be uncomfortable. When our trial continues to drag on for a while, we wind up going for comfort to things that were not meant to be comfort. This can be pornography, drugs, alcohol, sex, food, TV, sports, any old diversion will do. It can even be job; anything that keeps our mind off of what's going on.

It is, however, a perfect picture of the way things really are. In our "wilderness," we seek shelter and refuge from the circumstance of life, in the form of things that are **imitations of shelter or refuge**. The pitifully weak and

37

pathetic things of life become those things in which we put our trust. The weird part is that we humans can actually deceive ourselves into thinking that we are really receiving significant benefit from that which is not even close to a poor imitation of the real thing.

But to "sit down" had as much to do with his frame of mind as it did his physical exhaustion. Elijah had fallen from the pinnacle of success, with the thought that the spiritual direction of the country was finally back on course. Surely Ahab and Jezebel could not possibly ignore God's emphatic judgment. Certainly both would repent and things would change. His hopes, dreams, and prayers for the kingdom of Israel had at last been answered—but now this! This was the ultimate **disappointment.** Had he missed God in all this? Had he heard right? Had he done what God really wanted done? Or had he overstepped his bounds and presumptuously murdered 850 men and women, defiling the land one more time with their blood?

This series of events parallels another in the New Testament: when Peter and the other disciples had a really bad fishing trip immediately after Jesus's crucifixion. Nothing had gone like they thought it would; everything had fallen apart. Three-and-a-half years wasted. And here they were, having fished all night without catching a thing. What else could go wrong? Now, there was some dude yelling from the shore, "Fish on the other side of the boat!" What did he know? They'd been doing this for twenty years; they were professionals! They were so self-absorbed that they didn't even recognize Jesus' voice from the shore! We **self-medicate** very easily, and in our culture we can even get our local Doctor to medicate us if we can't figure out how to do it ourselves – and get insurance to pay for it in the process. It is that very thing that begins to seal the destruction of not only our relationships and our heart, but our relationship with the Lord as well.

One of the other reasons we choose to self-medicate is **shame**. It too is a function of our performance orientation taught to us by the system of the world and is appended to the old saw, "If I do right everything will be right." Up to this point Elijah could say that he had done things just as the lord had instructed, and all that worked out well, even if he hadn't enjoyed killing 850 men and women.

Yes, I said women, for the manner in which people worshipped in the temple of Asherah was via ecstatic sexual experiences with the temple prostitutes – men and women. As much as Elijah must have hated the practice, hacking the heads off dozens and dozens of women had to be a distasteful duty. He certainly didn't do it all by himself, for 850 people are not going to voluntarily line up for execution. Just being a part of it would have been traumatizing for anyone, including a holy man. Having to run for doing a righteous deed, even as difficult as it may have been, had to be shameful. Then to have to suffer the indignity of being hunted like a rabid dog for doing what God wanted was heaping shame upon shame.

Now I want to make a few other observations about Elijah's state of mind after forty-eight hours of flight into the wilderness. We've already suspected that he was frightened by his plight otherwise he would not have run off totally unprepared for this venture. He's **tired, hungry and angry** at what he's having to do after such a comprehensive victory over darkness that he's witnessed in Israel. He's angry at Ahab, angry at Jezebel and probably angry with God that he's in this position. So he plopped down uncomfortably under a big overgrown bush dejected. How the mighty have fallen!

In this place of solitude I'm sure he's reflecting on the event of the past few days;

- he is no doubt feeling **rejected**,
- **dejected** because his circumstance are so dire,
- **hopeless** because he knows the cavalry isn't coming, an early outgrowth of Psalms 13:12 *"hope deferred makes the heart sick."*
- **helpless** because he's all alone; actual or perceived loneliness is one of the principal motives behind self-medication and depression,
- **disillusioned** that God hasn't jumped in to save him,
- **discouraged** that this may well be how his life ends,
- **troubled** for the spiritual state of the nation, not to mention his own welfare,
- all his **insecurities** have been exposed,
- he is feeling the **indignation and injustice** of having to flee like a common criminal after having officiated at one of God's greatest judgment ceremonies ever,
- he would be feeling **betrayed,** for historically all of Israel's society, including its leadership, was based in a reverence and strict adherence to Jewish law and tradition, of which he (Elijah) had been a respected fixture.
- he is starting to become defined by his own pain,
- all his **expectations** have been dashed because neither the people, nor the nation's leadership have appreciated what he's done for them, and he's been the grand poo-bah of prophetic insight in Israel for quite some time,

- and he is presuming that his current circumstance is an horrific harbinger of his future – **abandoned** by God.
- The net result of it all is the seeds of **cynicism** are starting to sprout because even God hasn't seemed to take notice of what has happened or he's been through … after all he's done for him.

If you have ever been caught "between the rock and the hard place" for any length of time you have recognized each of these as having been something that you wrestled with in your own life. Unfortunately, it is all too common to each of us. As King David's son Solomon said in Ecclesiastes 1:9

> *"What has been is what will be, and what has been done is what will be done, and there is nothing new under the sun."*

When we are going through horrible trials and tribulations we have a real, although perhaps faint, expectation that God (you can read it as "the church" if you wish) is going to rise up and at the very least say something in your behalf, or reach out and do something for us to help mitigate the severity of our condition. When that doesn't happen we tend to blame them for "what they should have done." It is too easy to become cynical toward "them" as though they collectively should have known what we were going through and done something, even if we had no idea what that would have been. When expectations are dashed our judgment becomes a bit irrational because we can't see clearly (the ministry of confusion is still in effect) and consequently our ability to be understanding of others is virtually non-existant.

While working recently on my 17th book, *Dance Like You Mean It*, I went back through three or four of my most recent books to see if I was repeating myself in any way because some of these subjects can cause redundancy if I'm not careful. What popped out at me in a couple of instances was the harsh discovery of my own cynicism regarding the church was a bit too easy to identify, for I too am all too familiar with Elijah's frame of mind in the aftermath of his difficult situation.

Over the years my wife and I have played a prominent role in several smaller churches, in several startup churches and we were also on staff at of a church of about 350 for several years. I could tell you several stories of numerous Elder's meetings that went south quickly, the sticky fallout of gross misunderstandings and miscommunication, of having been either thrown under the bus on one or more occasions, or having been totally ignored in the midst of our pain – or all of the above at one time. I am sad to report that I apparently have allowed these negative experiences, while not life altering, to affect my view of the organized church. To make matters worse we have witnessed the lives of several others become toxic as a result of similar treatment, a couple of whom have created their own pet theology of suffering devoid of any redemptive message.

In suffering injustice, however great or small, we still have access to the power to make a choice in how we respond. The Greek stoic philosophers believed that in and of themselves, all circumstances are neither positive nor negative, but were in fact, neutral; that it was our choice which caused them to be viewed in one way or the other. While there is truth in that viewpoint, it is generally the magnitude of our pain that forces them to be colored as negative. Their reasoning was that each of us could enter a state through the strength and discipline of our own minds and the exercise of our will to choose to become impervious to it by intentionally choosing to accept it as positive.

As wonderful as that hypothesis sounds, I find that most of us allow fear to rob us of that capacity long before we are made aware that we could have made another choice, if indeed we ever saw it.

However, the other side of that stoic reasoning coin is in order for us to enter that state of mind and thus acquire that capacity to see everything as either neutral or positive, we must shut down our emotions in order to begin to experience it that way. That is not only unwise, but from my perspective it is tantamount to voluntarily shutting our heart down to every voice, including our own and the voice of our Father, in an effort to self-protect. That is totally counter to the way we've been created. We were created with emotions for a reason, for if we cannot feel pain neither can we feel joy … or love. The trick is to remain feeling and yet not become overwhelmed by them as Elijah did.

The key is not responding to fear and becoming overwhelmed by it as Elijah did, is partially to realize that fear is presenting us with an opportunity to either act on our own, or to trust that God can give us an appropriate response to it. Fundamentally, fear wants us to respond out of our automated soulish self-protection mechanisms, rather than rely on an outside source for the grace to respond in wisdom from our heavenly Father/

There is a cycle that we enter into when the invitation to fear is accepted. It produces shame for all the reasons previously cited; our performance oriented analytics kick in and tell us that we should have seen this coming and done something to prepare, we need to defend ourselves quickly and definitively, we can't let this go because if we do we'll be admitting guilt, etc. Shame produces control as a means of self-protection or preservation as an automatic response to an attack, which produces more fear. The cycle is self perpetuating.

The last part of verse 4 records that Elijah went one step further into the depths of depression:

He prayed that he might die.

If the enemy can't get you to commit suicide, then he'll settle for just making you miserable. Disappointment, disillusionment, and loss are some of the greatest enemies that we have to our personal security and sense of well being. Our personal security and sense of well being are founded in our assessment of our ability to control our circumstances and avoid disappointment and being disillusioned. Typically what happens is we fall into that place of being sorrowful about our situation when disappointment knocks on our door demanding our company. We feel sorry for ourselves that we are having to go through this, when seemingly no one else is – Oh, the injustice of it all! (See 1 Kings 19:10) Then the journey into the fullness of the depths of **depression** is relatively short.

What happens when you become depressed is that it affects you physically as well. When you become emotionally depressed, it robs you of physical energy, along with the desire to do anything that requires expending energy. You will begin to sleep more. Your diet becomes altered because you are no longer hungry because depression robs you of appetite, which has an adverse effect on the delicate chemical balance of your body. Then the stress you encounter becomes more difficult to handle. So you begin to sleep more and as a consequence, your abilities to fight back are decreased even further. Not only are you now living in denial, but mental clarity has evaporated and you no longer have the energy required to do anything about it. If you have chosen to also self-medicate then there are no longer any highs or lows, everything is the same blah and life becomes meaningless.

It's hidden from us in this story, but inevitably **anger** is always in play because we think we've done everything in our power to reverse our circumstances, so it's not our fault because God surely could and should have done something for us. But He chose not to. Anger never serves us well because it too is an element of pride.

Not to add insult to injury, but the end of verse four says:

So it's enough. Now Lord take my life.

If you stay in depression long enough, thoughts of **suicide** become a constant companion. It is the cowardly companion of hopelessness. This is really what the enemy is after. He knows why you're here and that scares the snot out of him. He cannot let you do what you're supposed to do or need to do. If you do, his kingdom cannot advance. If you connect with several others who are fulfilling their purpose, it can become contagious and he will lose a serious amount of ground. This is why he comes at us so surreptitiously and tries to separate us from those kind of relationships.

Another reason for this attack is that he not only wants to separate us from the support of others but if he can separate us from those whose lives we have been pouring into he can cause our lives to appear fruitless and without meaning.

He separated Elijah from the 400 young men whom he was mentoring through the School of The Prophets. Do you now have a sense of what the enemy was really after? He was after Elijah's **legacy**; his spiritual kids and grandkids. Later we find that Elijah's legacy was well represented by his spiritual son Elisha, whose spiritual exploits numbered twice as many as his mentor. The strategy that the enemy has for you is not only for you, but also for your kids is to break that multiplicative relationship that creates men and women who greatly prosper because of what you invested in them.

The attack is strategically formulated to be comprehensive. If you would bow to the enemy, he has an open door leverage your failure to attack those whom you lead. If you remember in Exodus 20, from which we get the 10 Commandments, the Lord says, "You'll have no other gods before me." None. Nada, Zip, Zero. Not even an image of them.

> "But if you do, *I will visit the iniquities of the Fathers upon the 3rd and 4th generation of those who hate me.*"

Why did he use that word 'hate'? If I will willfully allow the enemy to minister to me, it's as though I hate the Lord. I'm cooperating with the enemy. I'm sleeping with the enemy and he's ministering to me because I gave him permission to. And as I give in to the enemy, the iniquitous beliefs that govern my responses to the invitations of the enemy are then taught by example to those I have become a role model to.

Legacy is a big deal to God. If you doubt it, just look at the fruits of the mentoring relationship between Elijah and Elisha. That personal involvement, an investment if you will, produced a spiritual son that was able to work twice as many miracles as his spiritual father (mentor.) Just one more reason Jezebel is at work in our culture, and it may well be the greatest.

6

The Name

In this account, Jezebel is a Sidonian foreigner, the daughter of the king of Sidon, Ethbaal, whose name means "with Baal." Moreover, Sidon means "pride in their own glory." So, it is little wonder she found favor in the eyes of Ahab; they were two of a kind.

This is a clear picture of what we have become collectively in America. Individually and collectively, we have become a very prideful lot. *"Have it your way"* is more than a marketing gimmick to sell burgers; it's the national mantra of the self absorbed. I don't think there has ever been a time when Narcissism has gained as much attention as it has now simply because it has become so entrenched in the fabric of our society.

Consequently, we'll "marry" ourselves to all manner of things which are a mixture of good and evil, choosing to overlook the latter. Our former home of Asheville was no exception! The eclectic mix that is Asheville is amazing: tree huggers, dirt worshippers, goddess seekers, old hippies and gutter punks, travelers, Wiccans, New Agers, Buddhists, some forty-nine versions of Eastern mysticism, Christian cults, and a generous sprinkling of atheists and agnostics—all trying to get you to embrace the large population of lesbians and gays and an ultra-liberal agenda.

Now, although Jezebel was no Godly example before he married her, Ahab's failure to stand up for God on behalf of Israel cost him, and the country, dearly. That's the cost of personal pride. His Biblical epitaph now reads,

> *"Now Ahab, the son of Omri, did evil in the sight of the Lord, more than all who were before him."* (1 Kings 16:25)

Remember, even Moses was denied entry into the Promised Land because he failed to represent God properly before the people. Are you representing Him properly before your family? Your community?

This is a picture of what happens to a man who, when real success eludes him, he chooses to embrace the sensual in life. Jezebel was a worshipper of Baal and Asherah, the former worshipped by child sacrifice and the latter worshipped via temple prostitutes. A part of their worship was extreme sensuality, the height of which was sexual ecstasy with the temple prostitutes. Obviously, this got the better of a young king, and in the pursuit of it and association with it, he lead (or allowed) the country to fall into spiritual and financial ruin.

It has been my experience that Jezebel is not just any ordinary demonic entity, but probably a principality, or at least a Power, that is able to command other demons. We see the lust and perversion with which Jezebel and Ahab were associated. This is where our own national disgrace of abortion comes from. As a nation, we too have sacrificed entire generations of children at the altar of personal convenience. It's why we are encountering the first generation in history to have been raised by television. It has no morays, no boundaries, and will experiment with anything.

As my wife and I prepare to minister to people, we have them fill out a form which requires them to list all their sexual liaisons. For those thirty and under, we have found that roughly 30 percent will have had sexual relations with both sexes, and a few will have had sex with animals as well.

Asherah, which was the local goddess of fertility, was worshipped via temple prostitutes, both male and female. And this has become our own national fixation and has resulted in a level of perversion not seen since the Romans. We now have the first candidate for public office (August 2018) who if elected will lobby for a change in laws to make it permissible to have sex with children. We have become the world's largest purveyor of pornography and sensuality, and it's no wonder the balance of the world's population hates us for it.

Sensuality has always been an issue for humans. God made the human form beautiful for a reason. Without it, you and I wouldn't exist! But who needs a full color, full-page Victoria's Secret under garment ad with your morning coffee in the local newspaper, much less a similar commercial paraded before your teenage son on TV? We don't need any more hormones stimulated than we have already! The system is against you. These days it's not possible to find clothing for your teenage daughter that doesn't expose more of her anatomy than most parents are comfortable with.

The demonic entity Jezebel is encamped over this nation and we see the effects of its ministry on a daily basis – and our Ahab, the church remains silent.

Defeating Jezebel

7

Pornography: A Mental Affair

Reflecting back on chapter 5 and Elijah taking refuge under a bush in the middle of the wilderness we find one of the most prominent forms of distraction and self-medication that the enemy could ever have devised. Pornography is one of those *"high things that exalts itself against the knowledge of God"* (Romans 12:2). When the mind's eye begins to engage the unveiled female form, left unto itself, it cannot help but go to the next stage, fantasy. No one in his right mind would ever engage in a sexual fantasy with someone he couldn't control. What would be the point? So now the line has been crossed into control and manipulation. These are easily justified because, after all, they are just mental gymnastics—the victimless crime, so to speak.

But what is actually being experienced by the perpetrator, and may be interpreted as a control issue in a relationship, is actually rebellion by the mate. The spirit of a female is much more sensitive to fidelity issues than a male. And we are very different creatures. For instance, the male is sexually stimulated primarily via the eye-gate, while the female is sexually stimulated relationally.

How can she be so spiritually sensitive? Consider this: what was in the prayer of Jesus during His last night on the earth? What was so important? He had been with His disciples night and day for three-and-a-half years and knew that He was going to be cruelly tortured for the next eighteen hours. And He still had to pray to the Father for one last time. He prayed for unity! What was it that God declared important about the initial male-female relationship in Genesis? Unity—that they would become *one* flesh. The flesh is where we've understood the mind, the will, and the emotions reside, each of which is (or should be) subject to our spirit.

Now, don't get confused. Just because we can divide spirit, soul, and body for the purpose of definition, it doesn't mean that they are separate. For instance, if I am your dearest friend in the world and I betray you to your enemies and you lose your job, your house, and your car, will you not shed a tear? Will your body not experience gut wrenching pain? And after the pain is gone, will its memory not bring you pain? Will you not keep me at arm's length? Likewise, if I poked your wife or husband in the nose, would you not also desire to break mine? If married, we are connected as one. One area of your person cannot be impacted in a vacuum, without it impacting the remainder.

In the same way, God connected a man and wife to be one in all areas with each other. So, it should come as no surprise that when God-ordained unity is violated by a spouse, the other will experience a "disturbance in the force" and react negatively to it. The man cannot share himself with some other entity sexually, in reality or imagination, without it affecting his mate. She may not actually know what is going on, but I can assure you she is on the alert and her antennae are up and searching for the source.

Defeating Jezebel

We lived in the Atlanta area for fifteen years before moving to Asheville in 2002. A couple of years before we moved, a new magazine came out that got quite a lot of attention. It was published in a popular European format, on heavy stock, with a glossy slick finish; its subject matter was fashion and lifestyle. The name? *Jezebel*. Who were its principle advertisers? Six of the seven top women's underwear manufacturers/retailers. Just what the culture needs.

8

So What's Attacking You?

To review, Jezebel is not just any ordinary demon but a principality, able to command other demons. We know this by virtue of the collection of demonic forces arrayed against Elijah: intimidation, confusion, fear, lack, poverty, lust, perversion, isolation, pride, self-pity, depression, and witchcraft. Ephesians 6:12 says,

> *"For we wrestle not against flesh and blood, but against principalities, against powers, against the rulers of the darkness of this world, against spiritual wickedness in high places."*

There is a principle of Scripture interpretation, which applies here called the "Principle of First Mentioned." If the Bible presents to us a list, the first word mentioned is the most important, with respect to the remaining words. Satan never originated anything. So when he organized his kingdom, he patterned it after God's. He has generals, and he has foot soldiers (demons). We have been given authority over all the works of the enemy in the name of Jesus. In this case, the principality is not the one wreaking havoc in people's lives; it's the demons it commands.

Now, applying the principle reveals an order in the matter of spiritual warfare:

> Principalities
> Powers
> Rulers of darkness in this world
> Spiritual wickedness in high places

And if the same principle applies to Colossians 1:16, which says, "For by him were all things created, that are in heaven, and that are in earth, visible and invisible, whether they be thrones, or dominions, or principalities, or powers: all things were created by him, and for him," the list is slightly different:

> Thrones
> Dominions
> Principalities
> Powers

Finally, comparing Colossians 1:16 with Ephesians 6:12, provides a more complete list:

> Thrones
> Dominions
> Principalities
> Powers
> Rulers of darkness in this world
> Spiritual wickedness in high places

The good news? Now you know what you're up against! First Corinthians 15:46 says,

> *"Howbeit that was not first which is spiritual, but that which is natural; and afterward that which is spiritual."*

In other words, the earthly pattern which we can discern with our eyes is really a pattern of the spiritual. So what we see in the natural is generally what we can expect to see in the spiritual realm as well.

If the army of a foreign nation were to come against you, it would not send out its generals first but the privates and the corporals. They would be followed by sergeants, warrant officers, lieutenants, captains, colonels, and so on. But even general of the military are not the ones who declare war. It is the leadership of the country who fields the army that decides when and whom to declare war against. So we have to assume the satan, who is ultimately the originator of all this wickedness, is at the source of the attacks we experience.

If that's what happens in the natural, then we can expect the same thing to occur in the spiritual. You will win authority in the spirit by first whipping a few privates, then a few sergeants, then a few warrant officers, etc., defeating them all in succession until the entire "dark side" capitulates. Psalm 115:16 says,

> *"The heavens are the Lord's heavens, but the earth He has given into the hands of men."*

In spiritual warfare, as in natural warfare, after you have defeated everything the enemy has thrown against you, privates, sergeants, lieutenants, colonels, etc., the enemy either sues for peace or decides to pick on someone their own size. Since you have proven yourself to be so tough, the generals who are leading the whole mess will not come out after you.

Warning: Never attack a throne, power or principality head-on. You'll get whacked! Don't follow just any intercessor who thinks they know about spiritual warfare but knows little of how to conduct it other than screaming at them in the name of Jesus.

We were familiar with some folks who decided to take on the demons behind the local Order of Freemasons. They marched around the building praying and pounded on the exterior walls of the building with their fists for a while, then decided to go get coffee. Within 24 hours every single one of them in that group was sick in bed for two or three days. Yes, you could try to write it off as "there was just caught something that was going around" if you wish, but for all of them to catch it was a bit more than a mere coincidence.

If someone comes to you pronouncing that they see Jezebel in your church or on somebody you know or are in relationship with, do yourself a favor: just smile and walk away. Then pray for them because they'll need it! Bad!

It's for this very reason that you cannot defeat Jezebel in another's household, or in your church or social club. This is a battle they must win for themselves first, then you can help someone else win. I don't even recommend that a husband battle it over his own wife's life if she is not willing to fight it for herself. Once she has battled it for a couple of weeks or more, her husband may then join in to complete the battle over her, and for the entire household.

9

So Who's Really Attacking You?

In 1 Kings 19:2 we read, "Then Jezebel sent a messenger unto Elijah, saying, So let the gods do to me, and more also, if I make not thy life as the life of one of them by to morrow about this time."

Essentially, this is a declaration of war by a higher order demonic entity against Elijah in retaliation for the damage that he had just done against the 850 minions of the false religious gods set up in Israel by Jezebel. This declaration of war caused attack orders to be given to a large cadre of demons to be sent out in a specific order in an attempt to get Elijah to leave the ministry and commit suicide. The following is the laundry list of demonic beings operating under the broad ministry umbrella of Jezebel; these are the privates, etc. it has sent against you . . .

Intimidation. It's a direct challenge to your spiritual identity and authority. What was the first thing Satan tried with Jesus when he tempted Him in the wilderness? *You* have to understand that this spirit also understands your personality. It tries to drive you to react entirely in the flesh. If you are aggressive, it wants you to take it out on someone. If you are passive, it wants you to roll over and give up. Its strategy is to make your current list of problem loom larger than life and cause them to appear absolutely insurmountable.

Confusion. When we yield to intimidation, we automatically lose our ability to see the situation clearly and make correct decisions. The resulting lack of clarity often freezes people in the situation they are in, or causes them to begin to grasp at straws in an attempt to make something happen. Because pride is involved, blame shifting is a common result: *"If everyone else would just do what I know needs to be done, this would end!"* This spirit also tends to blind us to potential solutions or obscure things in a way that appears to remove access to potential solutions.

Lack of Discernment. Discernment is the ability to distinguish between good and evil. When we're being attacked for any length of time, this capacity is diminished and leaves us vulnerable to the enemy's plans. Without discernment we do some stupid things. I know a couple who made an incredible decision. They bought a new car on "faith." Now, faith isn't the issue here. What they wanted was. We know what we want, call it need, and presume that God wants the same for us. They made the purchase in spite of the fact that neither was employed. The husband was injured and could not work, and the wife had been a stay-at-home-mom with few skills. However, based upon the idea that they could sell their current auto they bought the car, started making payments but couldn't sell the existing car. The two payments squeezed them so hard they couldn't pay the electric bills. Then they got mad at God for the continual financial mess they were in. Without discernment, we can become terminally stupid.

Accusation. Satan is the "author of lies" (John 8:44) and
the "accuser of the brethren" (Rev 12:10). Therefore, any
attempt to intimidate is also implicitly accompanied by an
accusation. The accusation is always couched in a manner
that causes you to question your own personhood: who you
are at the core, your personal identity before God and man.
Since we are always our own worst critic and know every
place where we have failed and really screwed up, the
enemy takes advantage of it and turns a small shred of truth
into a federal indictment, which we willing make against
ourselves. And if there has been a problem with rejection in
the past, accusation will touch it again in a major way.

Flight. With any threat of intimidation there is just a hint of
the truth. Otherwise it would find no place in us to threaten.
When we bite the bait, the irrationality of the threat
becomes "our truth." Then self preservation requires us to
flee to a place of safety. For many, this has become
escapism on steroids. For those with self esteem issues or a
history of serious abuse, the feelings of being "trapped,
helpless/powerless, and hopeless" are all too familiar; flight
is automatic.

Manipulation/control. (This was Ahab's passive-
aggressive manipulation of his wife.) We will often resort
to extremes to protect ourselves, and logically that means to
do all we can to control our circumstances.

Lust. This comes from a couple of sources; Jezebel herself
who was sensual creature and the temple prostitutes who
had free access to the palace. Many have been known to
attempt to cover pain with satiating sexual desires, even if
it includes breaking covenants and breaking relationship
with those they love. When in their right mind, they have

no difficulty understanding the error of their ways, but they are powerless to do anything about it.

Fear. (Elijah feared for his life and ran from the problem.) This spirit somehow has the ability to touch that which is most insecure in our lives, thereby instilling fear—the fear of being known for what we really are and the fear of finding out that we may actually be unlovable, etc. When the door to fear is opened in our lives, the consequences become apparent. Hebrews 2:14-15 says,

> *"Since then the children are sharers in flesh and blood, he also himself in like manner partook of the same; that through death he might bring to naught him that had the power of death, that is, the devil; and might deliver all them who through fear of death were all their lifetime subject to bondage."*

Isolation or Separation. (Elijah removed himself from the palace by making a day's journey into the wilderness.) Often we are the ones who separate from others because of our own insecurities or the unanswered questions they raise. In our religious society financial success is equated to favor with God. The converse no one wants to talk about. We find ourselves voluntarily cutting ourselves off from the very people who can strengthen us and encourage us, or even correct our thinking. Elijah voluntarily cut himself off from "The King's Table." How many times have we done this to ourselves by continuing to keep an eye on the problem rather than the One that is the solution?.

Destruction of Communication. Following separation, the next area to be totally interrupted is our communication: communication with God, with one another, and honest communication with our own spirit. How often have we been able to lie to ourselves about our situation, its magnitude, and whose fault it is? When the wisdom of others does not temper us, "our truth" becomes "the truth."

Poverty/Lack. (Elijah left the place of God's provision and entered the wilderness.) This can be described as what I have already called having a hole in our bucket—there is never enough. When it looks like we're about to get ahead, along comes some emergency that sucks it all up. It can also be defined as excessive debt, which has no means of repayment. In the height of these situations, we can't seem to make a good financial decision even if one is presented to us. This can also be applied to poverty in all areas of life: a dry and lifeless relationship with God, empty personal relationships, no place of meaningful work or ministry, a lack of personal fulfillment, even in hobbies, or a lack of joy.

Pride. Pride can be described as looking at the problem and refusing to accept responsibility for it, while blindly trying to handle it alone rather than immediately turning to God. Remember, God disciplines those He loves. For men, pride can be a very difficult thing to deal with. We can compensate in many ways and can even hold up our efforts in ministry as proof that what we are doing is "of God" and doesn't need to be changed. Many have found that ministry is actually one of the most self-serving sacrifices that can be entered into and is simply a cover up for not dealing with the deepest of issues.

Weariness. If you've ever been in that situation you learned first-hand that the place you find yourself totally exhausted you are ripe for cratering in all areas of life and wisdom is very hard to come by. When you are exhausted and can't even rest because you didn't prepare for the journey, you are not only weary but you are miserable, making the entire experience unbearable.

Depression. (Elijah desired for God to end his life.) After a period where no prayer seems to be answered, the enemy comes to tell us that *"this is as good as its ever going to get."* Suicidal thoughts are often a common symptom. The presence of continual financial pressure always exacerbates every other problem we have and seems to suck the life out of everything else. Under these conditions, even a vacation isn't enjoyable because the thought of how you could use the money for sits right beside every activity that promises to be fun.

Self-pity. This is another element of pride—this was Elijah's assumption that he was the only man alive serving God, as he reflected upon his current, miserable circumstances. The failure of Elijah is also ours. His suffering was self imposed. He compounded his own misery by saying that he was no better than his father. He basically implied that he was a failure; he cursed himself by not honoring his father.

Surrender. (Neither Jezebel nor Ahab would fight, but Elijah dropped all his spiritual weapons.) After we have battled all the demons in hell, and even the hand of God, without success, rather than admit defeat we will simply sit down and do nothing.

Suicide. This reminds me of a lyric from a popular song from the 1970s: "Been down so long, Looks like up to me." This really is the ultimate goal of the enemy: to get us to give up on ourselves, God, and others, and take our own lives.

Consider also that the meaning of the name Jezebel is "non-cohabitant or unmarried." You could also throw in "independent." All of these demonic forces are geared to produce that one thing; to rob you of every life-giving relationship you have; to drive a wedge between you and all your relationships, even to the point of separating you from God Himself. Does it happen? You bet! When we sin, just like Adam and Eve, our first reaction is to run and hide. A spirit of shame will come to reinforce our guilt and further attempt to drive us from the presence of God.

10

A Warning from God

There is one other mention in the Bible of Jezebel. It comes from Revelation 2:18,

> "*And unto the angel of the church in Thyatira write; These things says the Son of God, who has eyes like a flame of fire, and his feet are like fine brass; I know your works, and love, and service, and faith, and your patience, and your works; and the last greater than the first.*"

Understand that Jesus is speaking to believers—and not just any believer at that! He is speaking to mature, productive citizens of the Kingdom. These are men and women who have been proven over time. These are men and women whose efforts are more productive now than previously— faithful men and women of the faith, of whom He is proud. Revelations 2:20 says, "*Notwithstanding, I have a few things against you, because you tolerate that woman Jezebel . . .*"

Basically, when, over time, there has been no apparent victory because God has not swept in triumphantly to change our circumstances, nor have our attempts at spiritual warfare brought any fruit, we get frustrated and give up. Essentially, we quit fighting the enemy and in so doing . . . embrace him—perhaps not whole heartedly but embraced nonetheless. This is often what happens when we fight and fight, battle and battle, pray and pray, and see no substantive result from our efforts. We grow weary in well doing. We voluntarily lay our weapons down. And in doing so, we agree—and thereby give permission—to the ministry of the enemy in our lives. We open ourselves and our families to whatever the enemy wants to bring against us, with our tacit approval.

If I wanted to steal your wallet from your purse or pants pocket and I came close to you and slowly reached in to take it, if you were in your right mind you would stop me. But if you did nothing, you would be "tolerating" my actions. By tolerating my actions, you would be tacitly approving of my attempt to rob you. Lack of opposition on your part means affirmative approval on your part, or, in other terms, giving me permission to "minister evil to you."

The bottom line is that by failing to fight the enemy on every front, we have given the enemy approval to rob us. When Jezebel declares war on us, it sends out a couple of dozen lower order demonic entities to attack us. When we do not immediately resist and continue to stand against them, we effectively give them permission to minister to us. And they are more than obliged to do so. The only way to turn the tide is to change our minds. The methodology for doing that follows.

11

The Ahab Spirit

Those who suffer from the ministry of Jezebel often suffer from the ministry of Ahab as well. I don't know how prevalent this spirit is in other countries, but it is a major one we deal with here in the United States. The reason is this: if you will not stand up to Jezebel, you will automatically agree with the spirit of Ahab. The Ahab spirit is usually discovered within the context of a marriage relationship at the peak of disaster, right before the relationship falls apart. It comes in a few different forms but is recognized as one of the following;

    A. The wife is controlling, manipulative, or overbearing, and the husband has given in to it, allowing the wife to run the marriage and the household.

    B. The wife is neither manipulative nor controlling, but by virtue of the fact that the husband refuses to take his rightful place as head of household, the wife is forced into it in order to provide a sense of order.

C. Or both have tendencies to be controlling and manipulative, but the wife has gained the upper hand because of the husband's time involvement with making a living or other outside pursuits that he has deemed more important. Given sufficient time, this situation too will fall into one of the above noted categories.

As a minister, you will usually be introduced to it when the spouse comes in for a prayer ministry session out of desperation to get the non-attending spouse 'fixed.' (It's usually the wife with the request.) The main complaint will be that there is no communication or intimacy in marriage.

I remember a couple that had been married for thirty-one years, and the wife had gotten to the point where she had no emotional feelings for her husband whatsoever. They both professed love for each other and were committed to making the marriage work but didn't know how, or where, to start to resurrect the deep emotional connection they had felt previously.

The major complaint was that their communication had become very superficial. He would not enter into a discussion of spiritual matters with her, and he had confessed to her that he seemed to have never been in touch with his own emotions and didn't know how to feel. When he wouldn't talk with her on a deeper level, she got angry with him. She told me that she had gotten over the need for sex over the last few years and had come to understand that she no longer needed his hugs either. Of course, he took that as rejection. It was a sad situation.

Pat and I personally went through a rough time when our own personal intimacy was at a low ebb. The difficulty reared its ugly head when we came to a point in our married life when she needed to know that she was valued, that she was worth something to me, that I would fight for her affections, and that I would defend her when she was under attack by outsiders. I was up for it but was totally clueless as to how to express (and/or demonstrate) these needs to her in a way that was meaningful and satisfying to her. The fact that (to my knowledge) no one was attacking her made me all the more clueless.

Part of our problem was that I was unaware of the fact that the Ahab spirit had closed in on me earlier in our marriage at an interesting time. We were in bed one night worshipping and praying, when the presence of Jesus came into the room. Pat stopped me mid sentence saying, *"Do you smell that? It's Jesus. Do you smell that?"* Well, I didn't smell a thing and said so. She kept on with expressions of delight that He had come in response to our prayers. I was nonplussed but said nothing. The issues that I had with my earthly father had left me somewhat miffed that I had been left out of this surprise visit. There were a few more such incidents that stole any zeal I had to pray with my wife at all.

When Adam watched Eve partake of the apple and chose not to intervene, the spirit of Ahab closed in upon him as well. Adam chose not to protect her or cover her in this encounter with the enemy. He could have stepped in at any time and cut it off. In fact, the coward was ready to watch her drop dead after eating the apple, just to see if what God had said was true about dying if they ate from the tree. When God asked what was going on, Adam blamed it all on her. Again, he chose not to cover, defend, or protect her. Instead, he took the easy way out. When God placed Adam in the Garden and gave him dominion over all creation, with it came the responsibility to care for it, protect it, nurture it, defend it, guide and direct it, and cover it with the authority God had given him. And this certainly included Eve as well.

You can't have dominion without automatically getting the responsibility that goes along with it. So, when we enter into a marriage relationship, the man is given the authority along with the responsibility to take dominion over anything that threatens his relationship or his wife. If somewhere along the line he chooses to lay down the responsibility, he's the only one who thinks it's okay. And God still holds him responsible. He hasn't removed his authority. He's just AWOL.

If he chooses not to fight for a way to express to his wife that he loves her, that he will defend her, that he values her, that he will encourage her in the areas of her insecurity, that he will cover her, that he will ruthlessly deal with the enemy on her behalf, he has not lost his authority, but he has set aside his responsibility. He may tell her that he loves her, but if he will not fight for her affections every day, she will have rough time reconciling what he says with the truth of what he does. And when the two don't line up, our humanity tells us to believe the worst.

Periodically, circumstances will arise to challenge our character. At some point in time, one of those things may be financial difficulty. If the male is the sole breadwinner, the temptation may be to let the wife deal with the creditors—to let her figure out how to keep all the balls in the air and how and when to "rob Peter to pay Paul." It's easy to justify because the man is out working and the wife is at home with nothing else to do but answer the phone. And she can't say anything more to them than the husband could. She may even be more persuasive. So, it even sounds like a good idea. But if the husband chooses to let her fend them off day after day, it will take a toll on her and the marriage relationship. The fact that the husband is not standing in as a shield for her says to her that he will not take his place of authority, that she is not valued, that when the chips are down he will not chose to defend her, and, in the end, he'll blame the whole thing on her.

When we look at the life of Ahab in 1st and 2nd Kings, we see a man who was the actual authority in the land—he was the king. But we see his wife taking all the action. He was obviously a man who feared failure, and so he let her—and perhaps even suggested that she—do all the dirty work. Because he abdicated his place of authority, she was forced to take it. Somebody had to lead! The problem is that when a man voluntarily abdicates leadership, the one it falls upon is not anointed for the task.

Genesis 3:16-19 says, *"To the woman he (God) said, I will greatly multiply your sorrow and your conception; in sorrow you shall bring forth children; and your desire shall be for your husband, and he shall rule over you. And to Adam he said, Because you listened to the voice of your wife, and ate of the tree, of which I commanded you, saying, You shall not eat of it: cursed is the ground for your sake; in sorrow you shall eat of it all the days of your life; Thorns and thistles it will bring forth; and you shall eat of the herbs of the field; By the sweat of your face shall you eat bread, till you return unto the ground; for out of it you were taken: for from dust you are, and unto dust you shall return."*

According to the Word of God, the result of the fall was that the woman's desire was to be for her husband and that he would rule over her. Further, she was to have pain in childbirth, and he was to have pain in causing the earth to bring forth its produce. But according to Romans 5:20, God grants us grace to accomplish those things that are given for us to do. So women have grace to love their husbands and to bear the pain of childbirth. And men have the grace to rule over their wives, as a protection for them and to accomplish work and provide for them and their offspring.

When the natural order of things is upset by a man not taking the authority given him, the same grace that is provided for the man is not there for the woman. When the roles are reversed, the woman no longer has the grace to love her husband that the proper God-ordained order provided. The husband no longer has the grace to rule (cover) over her. And the relationship suffers automatically.

When the order that God established has been reversed, there is no longer the God-given grace is no longer available to preserve the God-given elements that perpetuate the family order. So desire fails, order is perverted, conception is averted, and poverty enters. And it is a poverty of all things: love, acceptance, grace, sex, conversation, companionship, depth of relationship, happiness, and contentment.

Unless the man repents, asks forgiveness from God, and breaks the power of this spirit over his life, and assumes his proper role, the relationship will eventually fall apart. In order for this to be accomplished, a husband must deal with the authority issues in his life, break the power of fear and the man pleasing spirit, and renew his mind according to the Word of God.

In summary, I want to point to an issue related to the inter-connectedness between Ahab and Jezebel. You can't have one without the other. It might not appear that way, but there is a specific reason why God chose to include this story in the Bible—it's far more than just a part of the chronicle of the history of Israel's rulers. The events involving Ahab, Jezebel, and Elijah in 1 Kings are not presented in their correct chronological order actually. Logically, the issues disclosed in this narrative should also be included with the issues described in 1 Kings 21:4-6, where we see that Ahab is acting like a spoiled child who has not gotten his way. He wanted the neighbor's vineyard for his own because it was right next to his house. The owner refused to sell it, however, and Jezebel had him killed by using letters that she on behalf of Ahab.

So what are the issues revealed in this passage?

First, there is always some sort of unhealthy co-dependent relationship between an Ahab and a Jezebel. Each "needs" the other to get what they want, even if they have to manipulate each other, and others, to make it happen. As you are praying your way through these issues, ask the Lord to reveal to you where you may have adopted some co-dependent habits that you are not aware of or to clarify for you the depth of those of which you are not currently aware. I can guarantee you that if Jezebel and its minions have been ministering to you and your spouse for any length of time, this is an issue the two of you will have to resolve.

Second, when you sacrifice your morals/values to get what you want, you always get more than you bargained for. There is no Biblical discussion of how the marital alliance between Ahab and Jezebel came about, but we can logically assume that it was a quest for power on Jezebel's part and a desire to feel power on Ahab's part, which may have led to a mutual seduction.

The action which led to their mutual downfall was the manipulation of a bunch of local suck-ups into murdering Naboth for his field and also included violating a sacred principle in Israel—that of inheritance. (1 Kings 21) It was the law of the land in Israel that every seven years any property that was sold for less value than it was worth, or changed hands in payment of a debt or was not acquired by a family member, was to be "redeemed" by the former owner. This was set up so that there would always be an inheritance for the family in the form of the land through the family patriarch and, further, to ensure that no Israelite lands would ever end up permanently in the hands of a non-Israelite.

Land ownership was and still is a big deal to the Lord because He promised Abraham that Israel would be his and his descendants forever. The land was originally divided by tribe, then family group, and finally by individual family. It was intended for it to stay that way. Ahab and Jezebel had no such regard for the intentions or statutes of God, much less for the traditions of men. Samaria, where Ahab lived, was considered by Northern Jews to be the land of half-breeds because they had significantly inter-married and not chosen to keep their Jewish bloodlines pure. In many ways this casual treatment of "inheritance" was just another reason to hold them at arm's length. It was one of the reasons why Jesus' disciples reacted so significantly to his conversation with the Samaritan woman at the well.

Third, when the unhealthy are in power, corruption is always an ever-present and oh-so-willing companion. Evil powers must always collude with evil men in order to work out their evil plans. Such are the ways of evil men and women; they must find others as non-principled as themselves to do their dirty work so that they may continue to appear blameless. They seek one another out.

When God confronted Ahab through Elijah, the first thing Elijah said to Ahab was that he sold himself to do evil; he then told him that he was a murderer and a thief since Naboth was killed so that he could take possession of that which did not belong to him. In essence, God equated one deed with being as evil as the other. The interesting thing about a violation of "inheritance" (at least in this instance) is that the sentence of the Lord upon Ahab, following his repentance, was that the consequences of all Ahab's evil was to fall upon his own inheritance (his son).

12

Companions of Jezebel

Jezebel appears in one more incident in the Bible which is recounted for us in 1Kings 21and it may have repercussions in the fight we are considering. Even though the event we are about to look into is recorded in Chapter 21, and numerically follows Chapter 19, we do not actually know whether this event preceded or followed the events of 1 Kings 19:1-5. We do know that Elijah was the prophet in the land in both situations.

In this situation Ahab coveted a plot of land near one of his dwellings that had a rather large vineyard on it and Ahab went to the owner and asked him to sell it to him. When the owner said no Ahab offered to trade him for another plot of land. Again the owner said no because, as he said, he would never sell or trade away his inheritance – for even the Lord forbids that he should sell his father's legacy.

We may assume that the land had been in the family for a couple of generations and as is the case, grape vines do not produce a quantity of quality grapes for about six to seven years. When grape vines get to the age of twenty years or more they produce their best grapes because they have weathered brutal heat and withering cold which means that the roots are now well married to the land and the characteristics of the wine they can produce can be traced directly to it. As a side-note, if you have never tasted Israeli wines (specifically their reds) you are in for a gargantuan treat which in the future may cause you to throw rocks at the majority of wines from Nappa Valley, CA.

As a result of his definitive rebuff Ahab went home and pouted upon his bed. He didn't even go to dinner. Jezebel, puzzled at his behavior went to inquire of him and found that he was beyond consolation. Feeling sorry for her poor hubby she swore that she would get the vineyard for him, whereupon she hatched a plan to take care of Naboth and secure the vineyard for her husband.

So she wrote a letter and signed his name, sealed it with his seal, instructing the Elders and leaders of Naboth's (the vineyard owner) home town to proclaim a fast (certainly the religious thing to do). The instructions went on to say that they should find two sons of Belial (otherwise translated as "worthless men") and seat them across from Naboth and have them accuse him of cursing both God and the King, then have them take him out and stone him.

"His blaspheming God would be the forfeiture of his life, but not of his estate, and therefore he is also charged with treason, in blaspheming the king, for which his estate was to be confiscated, that so Ahab might have his vineyard." Matthew Henry's Commentary on the Whole Bible

That is precisely what happened. As soon as Ahab got the news from Jezebel that Naboth was now among the deceased (notice that he didn't ask how Naboth had met his end) he immediately took off to Naboth's house to secure his ownership of the vineyard. However, when the local prophet Elijah heard of it, stuff was shortly going to hit the fan! (1Kings 21:17)

Elijah surprised Ahab and quickly laid out God's judgment of his crimes;

> *1Ki 21:20-24 "Ahab said to Elijah, "Have you found me, O my enemy?" He answered, "I have found you, because you have sold yourself to do what is evil in the sight of the LORD.*
> *21 Behold, I will bring disaster upon you. I will utterly burn you up, and will cut off from Ahab every male, bond or free, in Israel.*
> *22 And I will make your house like the house of Jeroboam the son of Nebat, and like the house of Baasha the son of Ahijah, for the anger to which you have provoked me, and because you have made Israel to sin.*
> *23 And of Jezebel the LORD also said, 'The dogs shall eat Jezebel within the walls of Jezreel.'*
> *24 Anyone belonging to Ahab who dies in the city the dogs shall eat, and anyone of his who dies in the open country the birds of the heavens shall eat."*
> *(ESV)*

Ahab meets his pitiful end in 1 Kings Chapter 22 and Jezebel meets her doom in 2 Kings Chapter 9 just as Elijah said; the dogs licking their blood.

I have not had the misfortune of having evil, worthless men make up lies to discredit me and rob me of property or position, but I have known those that have. It is an especially difficult thing to weather and the reason I have included it here is not only to show you the lengths to which this spirit will go when it declares war on you, but to remind you that you have a kinsman redeemer who is able to save. Often we are so overwhelmed with the attack and the belief that good will prevail that we forget this is a war and frequently there is collateral damage as a result of it. An appeal to the Courts of Heaven is about the only defense you can mount in such cases. Do not abandon your position for it will insure a loss.

13

The Battle for Restoration

Here is a practical way to work toward defeating Jezebel:

- Pray through 1 Kings 19 and take a personal inventory of all of the spirits afflicting you by looking at the symptoms they have produced in your life. Your circumstances will be the key to seeing what's going on. Ask the Holy Spirit to bring you revelation on all the ways the enemy has been able to minister to you through by studying what Elijah went through. Elijah went from being the prophet to his nation to a prophetic man with no one to prophesy to (loss of personal esteem); from a man who was head of the School of the Prophets to a man whose only company was a raven (isolated and cut off from support); from a man who could enter the King's palace and dine with him anytime he wanted to a broken fellow alone in the wilderness (poverty and lack); and Elijah had a servant who was conventionally connected to him and yet was alone (isolated and disconnected from life giving relationships). What would such a place do to you? Put

Tues. 3/9/21

Defeating Jezebel

yourself in his place; emotionally it would be hard, and
physically it would be difficult. List them here;

grief	rejection
depression	pride
self-hate	arrogance
suicidal thoughts	vanity
resentment	greed
bitterness	idolatry (work, shopping)
self-pity	adultery
isolation	(fantasy)
fear	lust
denial	mental illness
self-medication/addiction	
distractions	contempt + disresp
busyness	obesity weight gain injury
insomnia / difficulty sleeping	

catastrophic thinking "something's always wrong"

- exhaustion
- strife

- accidents
- infirmity
- incubus
- divination
- unbelief

Control + manipulation
murder
shame

jealousy
envy
defeat
despair

- Verbally ask forgiveness from God for participating
with all these demonic forces and for allowing them to
minister to you for so long (see Revelation 2:1-5).

82

- Break any and all agreements, whether written, verbal, or implied, with each demonic force. Break the agreements/contracts with each one in turn, by name. This includes the spirit of Ahab because he represents a prideful, spineless slime-ball who didn't stand up for anything (see Matthew 11:12). Submit each area by name to the authority of God and the Lordship of Jesus Christ. It may sound something like this: *"Father, in the name of Jesus, I repent for allowing X to minister to me. I break every place of agreement with X and cancel any contract or permission I gave X, whether written, spoken, or implied by my action or inaction, to continue to minister to me. This dance is done! I take that ground back and give it to the Lord Jesus Christ to rule and reign over."*

- Do this at least three times a day *out loud*, more if you can, for thirty consecutive days or more. At the end of the thirty days, you *will* see a difference in your condition!

- Get mad: yell, scream, and throw stuff at your enemies if you have to for the first week. This is not normal behavior for a believer because, according to the Word, the Kingdom of God is a Kingdom of peace. But you may need to be stirred up from lethargy to pick up your weapons and fight again.

- The next thing you will have to engage is your pride! Typically it will take another member of the body to help you focus in on some specific actions to take here. Understand that pride dies hard, and the action you may be called to take may be difficult. But remember, that

God resists the proud, and you don't want to continue in this path because it keeps you out of the "place of grace."

- Break guilt and shame from yourself, or have someone you trust to do it for you as you release yourself from guilt, shame, self-condemnation, etc.

- Understand that somewhere in the seven to ten day time frame the enemy will come to the conclusion that if a counter-attack is not mounted soon the battle and the war will be lost. It will act to try to recover the ground that it has thus far lost. Do not be afraid, because the counter attack will be so lame it will be laughable and easily recognized because now your eyes will be open to things you could not see before. It will likely even seem to be a really stupid attempt, but falling for it will put you back where you started. Just be aware that it will happen and ask Holy Spirit to make sure you don't miss it.

You must also understand that this spirit will attack you off and on throughout your life-time. It will never give up. But once defeated, what once took you thirty days to recover can now be accomplished in three hours or less.

Remember that the enemy usually attacks you at your point of destiny. Just because you defeated him this time, do not expect that he will never again come to test your authority or resolve. The hate that the enemy has for you and God is never ending. Just as hate is irrational in human beings, the defeat the enemy just suffered is a guarantee that he will come and try that same door again. Don't let that scare you. If you defeated him once, you can do so again. The Word says that we are not ignorant of the enemy's devices (see 2

Corinthians 2:11); therefore, the enemy will not gain an advantage over us. Fore-warned is fore-armed. The cool thing is that because you will have some experience behind you, the next encounter will be much easier.

Essentially what you're doing is canceling the ministry of these demonic entities against you and putting Jesus Christ in the place that He belongs in your life every day.

The prescription was to do this for 30 days, and I think it was probably 40-45 days later when a gal came to me at church and said, "I run an assisted living facility over in Roswell and I need a maintenance guy. I know you have a facilities background and I think you'd fit in well. Would you like to take it? All I can offer you now is $32,000 a year."

At the time I was working for Chic-fil-A opening the store at 4:30 in the morning for the cooks who were making 3 times what I was. So when she made me that offer it was not difficult to come to a quick decision. I went to work for her the very next week. Then a few months later she came to me and said, "Jim, you've done a good job here. We really appreciate it. And especially in an environment where it's virtually all women in this profession, you have brought a stability here that we really greatly appreciate. I've decided I'm taking the regional vice president's job and I'd like to offer you mine. All I can offer you now is $61,000 a year. Would that be okay?"

Uh, duh. "Yeah let's do this."

Everybody that I've taught this to in the last 18 years or so, who has faithfully practiced it, has had something very similar happen occur in their lives.

In Revelation 21, the Lord says,

> *"I am the God who makes all things new. Write this down for it is faithful and true."*

We have to put Him in the place He belongs in our lives if we are to expect all things to become new. Not only did things change for us financially, but there was almost an immediate restoration of the communication between my wife and I, partially because the stress was lifted, but mostly because the demonic oppression was lifted and Jesus was back in the driver's seat.

The reality is that you and I have an enemy. He's mad at you and he's mad at God. He's mad at you because you bear the image of the God who threw his butt out of heaven. He's trying to take it out on you so he can get back at God. It doesn't make any difference if you're rich or poor. You're a perfect target. His ministry is indiscriminate.

But there's one thing that will stand between you and victory in the Lord. When we buy into this thing, not only do we isolate, but we enter into denial. If I am unwilling to say, "I have a problem." If I am unwilling to say, "I'm in pain. This hurts. I'm confused. I don't know what's going on. I don't know how to get out of this thing. Help me." You'll stay in it.

Pride not only prepares the fall, but it will keep you in the place you fell.

Part of the interesting thing about this whole deal is you can't have a Jezebel without an Ahab. Ahab is pride. Somewhere in this solution that the Lord brings you, h

He will deal with your pride. He's not going to cut you off at the knees, but you will have to bow your knee. He will not abide pride. Pride says, "I'm still the God of my own life. But I want you to do it anyway. Fix it." He's not up for that.

This tool is useful in the battle against all kinds of other spiritual attacks, but one of the cool things about it is that once you have defeated this thing, by just putting the Lord back into the place that He belongs, you'll not immunize yourself against attack from the enemy. Just because you beat him once, his pride will not bow. He's going to attack you again. But the reality is, once you've done it, it's really easy to see it coming again the next time. You don't have to suffer for a long time because you will realize, "Oh gosh, this is a familiar mess. I need to do something about it."

14

In Conclusion . . .

I want you to understand that in religious circles so much has been made of the Jezebel spirit that when the name is mentioned the mind automatically assumes that people are saying that someone has a Jezebel spirit in them, on them, or operating through them. We never stop to think that this spirit has a mind of its own and can attack anyone it desires in a blatant attempt to destroy their lives. This isn't about what they have; it's about what's attacking them and how to defend themselves against it and overcome it!

I also want you to understand that the Church has thrown around the term Jezebel as a weapon, usually in the context of labeling someone as a Jezebel, or having the spirit thereof as a means judging a female, who has a strong personality and may be immature in her gifting. It has usually been reserved for such women; strong willed, opinionated, with a strong personality and the gift of discernment. The insecurities of the religious bear can be provoked quite easily.

89

Frankly, this sort of response is often a gross misapplication of the Word for the sake of convenience because a principality is not going to attack someone just to pick on them. Demons are extremely prideful and would not stoop to do anything that can be done for them by another demon that is subject to it. So to label someone as a Jezebel is not only to expose ignorance, but it is to also fall head over heels into judgment of another person.

People can operate under a spirit of control, or be controlling and manipulative, even vindictive when offended, without being under the influence of Jezebel. A perfect example is a woman we ministered to in England who was crying that her marriage was in trouble because her husband would not back her up in a conflict with her daughter in-law. She couldn't understand why her daughter-in-law had stopped speaking to her when she had repeatedly given her advice about a chronic health issue that was blocking her from getting pregnant. The husband simply wanted her to be quiet and let them work it out for themselves.

The real issue behind this flap was that her son had married a woman fifteen years his senior and his mother was afraid she would not have any grandchildren because of the chronic health problem. So, she was interjecting herself into a sensitive situation where her advice wasn't welcome. The woman wasn't operating under Jezebel, or a controlling spirit; rather, she was just desirous of grandchildren and wasn't being the least bit sensitive to her daughter-in-law's feelings, nor open to wisdom in how to handle it. She had not been able to put the issue into God's hands. She had elevated her selfish desires above the right of her son and daughter-in-law to govern their own lives and do what they felt was best for them.

Defeating Jezebel

The real difficulty behind most accusations of Jezebel is the lack of ability to confront someone with a strong personality and tell them the truth in love. Just because someone is a "pain in the butt" doesn't mean Jezebel is involved. It's easier to get mad, separate from them, and justify your own sorry attitude and lack of guts by labeling them as being driven by some foul spirit. So before you go paste that name on anyone, pray about it with an open mind. It may just turn out to be your issue and not them at all.

Let me also add that there is still a foul spirit in the Church that it has embraced for centuries; the subjugation of women. It requires them to step out of their place of effective ministry to make way for a man, even if he's unprepared and totally un-anointed. A recent argument I heard was, *"women only held places of authority because men would not step up. Now that men are stepping up, women need to sit down and shut up. Anyone that will not is operating in a Jezebel spirit."*

Well, if there's one thing that causes the "spirit of slap" to rise up in me and an overwhelming desire to "minister" through the sudden "laying on of hands," it's this kind of arrogant, pompous posturing! How dare anyone give in to the plans of the enemy and disqualify 50 percent of the Body of Christ in one wave of the hand! This isn't Jezebel; this is the spirit of stupid driven by misogyny! So if this thing is flying around your local body, call it what it is and pray!

Don't get me wrong. I'm not advocating for women to become the head pastor at every local congregation. But what I am saying is that I have met many women who from a ministerial point of view are more qualified spiritually than many of their male counter- parts who have been named deacons and elders in the local church. But it certainly seems stupid for us to disqualify half of the Body of Christ from serving in high responsible and effective positions just because they are females. (That certainly sounds like something the enemy would want us to do.)

For far too long we have been ignorant of the enemy's devices. But praise be to God because He is still in the redemption business!

Defeating Jezebel

House of Healing Ministries

office@houseofhealingministries.org
www.houseofhealingministries.org
www.traumaprayer.com

Jim and his wife Pat, have been doing inner healing and deliverance for the better part of 35 years, the last 16 of which have been full time. They founded House of Healing Ministries in 2003 and spend about half their time meeting with individuals for inner healing prayer ministry one-on-one in a safe, comfortable environment of their private office. The balance of their time is spent traveling, teaching and training others to become effective in the inner healing and deliverance tools they impart as a part of healing communities all across the US.

Personal ministry is available for a fee at $125 per hour. For those who are experiencing financial hardship they will minister based upon the receipt of love-offerings so that ministry is available to all regardless of their financial situation.

If you would like to contribute to their efforts, or become a monthly supporter please visit their web site www.houseofhealingministries.org for more information. In the context of personal ministry you will receive healing, but you will also learn to help others as you have been helped (or comforted; see 2 Corinthians 1:4).

Defeating Jezebel

If you would like to schedule a training event, or a private ministry appointment, write, e-mail or call (contact information is above).

Be sure to check into other books by Jim Banks available at Amazon.com;

The Effects of Trauma and How To Deal With It, 3ʳᵈ Ed
A Workbook for the above title
One Calling, One Ministry
Cast A Long Shadow
Find Your Life Calling
Hope for Freedom
Finishing Well
Helping Your Veteran Deal With The Effects of Trauma
The Insidious Dance, The Paralysis of Perfectionism
Dance Like You Mean It
Sex Trafficking Ministry Manual w/ Becca Wineka
Angels and Demons
The Enemy Within
Boundaries
Choose Your Outcome w/ Mandy Valdes
Just Thinking

Made in the USA
Coppell, TX
20 December 2020